Taking Care

of Your Subaru

The Ultimate Subaru Owner's Guide

Thanks for being a great customer and I hope you enjoy the book!

Kurt Adler

Taking Care

of Your Subaru

The Ultimate Subaru Owner's Guide

What You'll Learn By Reading This Book:

- ➢ Car Care Basics

- ➢ Tips on Buying a Vehicle

- ➢ The Truth About Extended Warranties

- ➢ A "How To" Section

- ➢ How AA the Shop got Started

Taking Care

of Your Subaru

The Ultimate Subaru Owner's Guide

First Printing: September 2014

ISBN-13: 978-1500809904

Kurt Adler
A&A The Shop
4617 Old Seward Hwy,
Anchorage, AK 99503

(907) 562-3919

www.AAtheShop.com

www.PaperbackExpert.com

Customer Testimonials
(read others at our website)

A & A The Shop is always honest and trustworthy. In the three years I've been a customer of theirs, I've only ever had really good experiences. They are helpful and never do any work I don't need done. They are great.

Tracy W.

I have been using A & A The Shop for 7 years now. I know they're in the auto business but what I tell people is that they're in the trust business. Everyone I talk to who has a Subaru goes to them.
They service my car every 3,000 miles, and my car currently has 160,000 miles on it. I have been very satisfied with the service.

Brian G.

They know my name every time I walk in the door. I have considered never switching out of a Subaru because I love the service at A & A The Shop. They are truthful and honest. They will recommend something to be done, and I will ask if it needs to be done now or after awhile. They will tell me if I need to do it now or if it can wait and tell me the consequences of either choice.

I have been using them for at least the last 5 years. The service is always fast, professional, and reasonably priced. I hate going to the dealer and would rather go to A & A The Shop.

Christie V.

The service is great. The employees are genuine and professional. The quality of work is extraordinary. I have made many referrals to my friends and not been disappointed by any feedback. The A&A Shop is a delight for Subaru lovers.

Lisa G.

I've been coming here easily for over 10 years and they have kept my '92 Legacy in awesome running order ever since. If you have a Subaru this is the shop to go to!

Linda F.

Kurt has always been very forthright with me and upfront about what's going on. They are knowledgeable about what they're doing, and their knowledge goes above and beyond what the dealership can tell you. If there is ever any problem, they always take care of it. I would encourage others to take your cars to A & A The Shop. They have A+ service.

Robin P.

Table of Contents

www.AAtheShop.com

My Background

I come from a family of geologists and engineers. My dad is a geologist, as is one of my brothers. My sister is an engineer, and another brother is a mining engineer. From the time I was a small child, our nightly dinner conversation centered around their work. This "shop-talk" about minerals and the different ways of mining them inspired my own interest in prospecting.

In 1980, at the tender age of 16, my life took a dramatic turn when our family moved to Alaska. The next year, my father arranged for me to go into the bush with a real prospector. We trekked to a place called Tofte, a historic mining area not far from Manley Hot Springs, northwest of Fairbanks, and stayed

Kurt during his prospecting years

in a log cabin while working there. My particular job was to take pan samples and pan for gold and tin—work I found intensely interesting.

After graduating from Service High School in Anchorage, I couldn't decide what I wanted to do as my life's work. Initially, I explored the field of mining engineering, then chose to go into welding, instead. After attending classes in welding, I received my certification.

I worked as a welder until I could save enough money to buy my own tools, truck and equipment to work as a mechanic. I then took classes in auto and diesel mechanics. However, when I graduated, I decided to pursue my previous interest in prospecting. Back into the field I went, working as a prospector.

Kurt doing some prospecting

There, in the Circle Mining District and in the Brooks Range, I was able to work with my family, observe many mining operations, and prospect alongside various miners in these small outfits. Our job took us throughout most of the state of Alaska. We ran geophysics to keep small, family miners on their pay streak. This allowed them to mine their claims more efficiently and economically, and to lessen environmental impact. Our family operation still exists today and my father, at the age of 77, works every day, though the company operation is run by my brother, Kevin.

Cominco Alaska was my next employer. They hired me for their exploration department. With a helicopter, a pilot, and a mechanic we flew across Alaska doing regional exploration and sampling for the company's geologists. Our team worked

Kurt exploring parts of Alaska

prospecting target sites, gathering samples, and following up with geochemical surveys and/or geophysics. If these ventures proved successful, we staked claims and worked to prove up the ground. I also had exciting opportunities to work in the Altiplano in the Atacama Desert in Chile and built exploration camps for mineral exploration near Magadan, Russia.

What does this have to do with my current profession in automotive mechanics? A friend from my classes in auto and diesel mechanics, Don Boston, started a Subaru business and asked me to become a partner with him. Since I was still prospecting, I declined.

It wasn't until I met my wife-to-be, Joan Vallie, and was called to the married life that I gave up the wandering life of a prospector and settled in Anchorage. Seeing my wife (an exploration geologist, by the way) maybe two months out of the year just wasn't the kind of life I wanted anymore.

The following year, I went to work for a man I really respect, Kyle Brown, owner of Discovery Drilling in Anchorage. He helped me brush off the rust of my vocational skills, putting me to work welding, fabricating, helping with geotechnical drilling, and mechanical work.

During that year, my wife became pregnant with our twin daughters, Paige and Danielle. That year I decided to go to work for Don Boston. My wife gave birth to our twins the same week I went to work for Don. Believe me when I say it was a very exciting and nervous time in our lives because we had given up over half our pay to join into a budding new company. It was a part of my life I will never forget—like jumping into the deep end of the pool without knowing how to swim! The next year I became a partner in AAA Subaru, a very small operation with only four employees. Back then, we worked in a one bay shop, without lifts, that you could barely fit two Subarus end to end.

Let me just say it was very basic—and cold. In the winter, there were times we worked *inside* the shop in temperatures at or below 10 degrees F. A year before I joined them, they worked off a 100' extension cord, a generator, a drop light and a 55-gallon barrel stove to put out what heat it could. I helped install electrical and the heating systems.

Things gradually improved as more customers heard about this hole-in-the-wall Subaru shop that did quality work for a reasonable price. It was no time at all before we had so much business we sometimes had to work outside on cars in the Alaskan winter.

In the early days, most of our clientele were college students and people who really didn't have a lot of money

6

to keep their cars going, so we became that go-to shop where they could get good work at reasonable prices. We weren't a high end shop, of course. We had to work with used parts most of the time back then, but we helped many people who couldn't have afforded to have their vehicles repaired, otherwise.

In 1998, we purchased another building about a block from our old facility. The new building had seven bays—about 5000 square feet. It was a palace compared to the old place.

We eventually opened multiple shops, but expansion pains and logistical obstacles convinced us we needed to downsize. As a result, Don Boston and I decided to split the business in 2004. I bought his interest in the Anchorage shop and he got the Soldotna shop.

From that point, I took on a new partner, my wife. She has been instrumental in helping me run a successful business and we couldn't be happier. We changed the name to A&A The Shop. It stands for Adler and Adler.

My wife and I opened a secondary location in Eagle River in September of 2013 when Dave Miller, an independent Subaru technician for over 30 years, decided to retire. He wanted someone with honesty and integrity to buy his business and to provide his lifelong friends and customers with continued excellence. Believe me, we feel honored that he felt confident enough to allow us to take over that responsibility.

Dave maintained a small but great facility that really fit the great Eagle River community and we intend to continue it and make it even better. Our Eagle River shop is currently managed and operated by Zack Barnett, a master certified ASE (Automotive Service Excellence) technician who's been with us seven years and has undergone extensive specialized training in advising customers on maintaining and repairing their Subarus.

So now, we offer two great locations with ten dedicated technicians and three service advisors to provide the exclusive maintenance and repair on Alaska's car of choice, Subaru.

That's one element that sets us apart from other businesses and makes us unique. We love Subarus. We love the way they drive, how they're wired, and the way they run in the cold—especially up here. They have a perfect weight-to-power ratio so they can drive through snow like no other car on the market.

That gives us the unique advantage over all other shops that have to concentrate on many other car and truck models. We save our customers time and money because we know these cars so well, we readily see the trouble spots.

The best part of our business, though, is that it's like being in one big family. We like to think we are taking the same care we would if we were working on our mom's car. We know our customers have a choice of where they do business and we're happy they've chosen us. We'll do our best to maintain that trust.

Subaru got their start in the United States in Philadelphia in 1968. But the biggest market success for Subaru in the US quickly became the mountain states where the winter driving conditions made the all-wheel-drive Subaru the car of choice. They perform in cold and snow in any terrain. They do it because of their superior traction and their ability to shift into "four high, four low." It's almost like driving a little truck. Subaru has its own fan club; people who buy them rarely drive anything but Subaru.

Since we're Subaru specialists, we can quickly diagnose problems. Because of that, our customers save both time and money. We know our stuff! With this kind of confidence, ability, and foresight, we're able to increase the warranty on our work to 36-months or 36,000 miles. It's better than a 24-carat gold warranty!

We know Subarus. We're ASE certified, and most of my mechanics and technicians have been with me for over ten years. They know what they're doing. That's why we can offer such a strong warranty.

One analogy I use is the difference between a general practitioner and a brain surgeon. If you've got a brain tumor, the brain surgeon can help you more than the GP. It's the same with us. If you have a Subaru, it just doesn't make sense to take it to anyone else. Do you want someone who's seen 10 Subarus this year, or someone who's seen 2,000?

Being an expert in anything takes time, perseverance and hard work. We've done these things, so we have the qualifications, certifications, knowledge and expertise to achieve our goal—to provide the best possible service for our customers. Because of that, many of our customers have "grown up" with us. They started coming to us when they were young kids with their first Subaru.

We've watched them throughout their lives since then—the graduations, weddings, births, job changes and promotions. That's gratifying to my wife and me, as well as our technicians. It's gratifying to our customers because they know they can rely on us to properly take care of them, fix their car right, and then, of course, there's the gold standard warranty behind everything we do.

We are a service-oriented business. We never lose sight of the fact that, without our customers, we'd have no business! Sounds like a simple statement, but it's amazing how often businesses lose sight of that. And when I'm on the receiving end, I can sense it, too. We *enjoy* making our customers happy.

Why I Wrote This Book

The automobile was designed to replace the horse. That's why it was originally called the "horseless carriage." It has succeeded in its original goals—it gets us where we want to go faster than horses and makes our work much easier.

In the early years, cars were such a big deal that the men who owned them wanted to learn everything there was about their vehicle. Most people knew how to take care of them, too. And each car seemed to take on the owner's personality.

You could see a car coming toward you, and would know exactly what kind of car it was. There weren't that many makes and models on the road back then.

Things have certainly changed. Currently, there are approximately 44 different nameplates with 211 different models to choose from—and endless numbers of sub-models.

Technology advances so rapidly now that a complete understanding of your car is nearly impossible, unless you live and breathe it as I do. People tell me they used to be able to look under the hood and know the name of every part they could see. Today those same people will not even raise the hood—they're too scared and intimidated to look! Most of my customers admit they'd love to know more about their cars. That's why I wrote this book.

My heart desires to serve people, to help them in any way I can. If someone in need crosses my path, and I have the resources to meet their need, I don't just say, "go be warm and be fed." Instead, I want to serve them, to help them, to meet their need, if I can.

I see a need for people to know not only how to take care of their car but to gain wisdom when they replace it with a new or used one. So here it is—the self-help book of car ownership that you can link to self-help videos on our website. It won't make you a Master Certified auto mechanic, but it will help you better understand how to keep yourself, your family, and your car safe.

Safety is a primary objective every time we get in a car. We pray for travel mercies. We tell our children to drive safely. Road signs tell us to drive safely, to wear our seat belts, and obey traffic laws—all so that we will "arrive alive" at our destinations.

Cars were never meant to be phone booths, texting stations or music halls. They were meant to help us arrive safely.

Most of the advancements in technology have an underlying theme of safety, many of which are addressed in these pages. More importantly, this book provides simple, helpful information on car ownership. Armed with this knowledge, understanding the warning signs, and knowing what to do when things go wrong will help us stay safer in and around our automobiles.

So consider me the "dad you never had" who desires you to know how to care for your car and arrive safely. If you have a specific question, simply go to www.AAtheShop.com. Let me know how I can help.

Kurt Adler
Owner of A&A The Shop
May 2014

Kurt Jokela during the 2005 Serum Run

Kurt Adler during the 2005 Serum Run

Cold-Weather Driving Tips

Speaking of experts, Alaskans are savvy when it comes to driving in cold, snowy, winter weather. So I wanted to pass a few tips to the reader that might come in handy. For one thing, crazy shifts in temperatures are hard on vehicles. If it's warm one day and freezing the next, it sometimes reduces their ability to perform.

a) *Make sure your car is properly, and regularly, serviced. This is my most important piece of advice!* The last place you want to be in these kinds of temperatures is broken down on the side of the road. (Our customers do a good job with this. In the past 15 years, we've gone from earning around $3000/month for towing to $300/month.)

- Not only do you need regular oil changes, but your coolant must be checked, as well. That's another reason it's so important to get 15,000, 30-, 45-, 60-, 75-, 90,000 miles services done. Postponing servicing costs you money—in fuel efficiency as well as wear and tear on your engine.

b) Make sure your battery stays fully charged.

- If you live in a cold-weather state, you need a winter battery. Winter batteries possess a higher cold cranking amperage than regular batteries.

- Use a battery blanket (like an electric blanket for your battery) when appropriate.

- If you drive only short distances, your battery may not have time to fully charge, especially if other things draw against it—like windshield wipers, heater, etc. So once a week, take your car for a longer drive so the battery can fully charge.

c) Avoid potholes and rough surfaces, especially when it's cold outside.

d) Give your car at least two minutes to warm up before you begin driving or turn on the heater. Cars have multiple computer sensors today—coolant temperature sensor, O2 sensor, barometric sensors, etc. They don't begin to send the proper signals until things warm up a bit. Failure to allow the car to warm up properly can cause runnability issues, as well as lower fuel economy.

So if you are from one of the cold-weather states, these tips will help you save money, stay safer and help your car perform better. I can explain in detail *why* each of these suggestions will benefit you, but I won't go into the scientific data at this time. If you're interested in learning more, see the appendices at the end of the book.

When Is It Time to Replace My Car?

My philosophy is that if you budget regular maintenance on your vehicle, it will pay you dividends in the number of years it will perform for you. Replace the little things now, or be forced to replace the big things later.

People who don't take care of their cars sometimes face those large bills and think, "I'll just get a new car!" When you calculate the maintenance cost versus the new car cost, it's radically different. So my advice is that doing the maintenance now will help you avoid the cost of buying a new car later.

A friend of mine put on his website, "Save $34,000." That got a lot of attention! His point was that you can save the price of a new car by maintaining your existing vehicle, thereby giving you added years of use. With Subarus, what we've seen is that our customers are getting 160,000 to 180,000 miles and still going strong. I have several customers with over 400,000 Alaskan miles on their Subaru, but the grand prize winner has 547,000 miles and still going. These cars still run great because they've been so well maintained. And let's face it—up here, those aren't easy miles!

So when *should* you think about replacing your car? When the age of the car prevents me from finding adequate parts to repair them, it's time to start thinking about another one. So I tend to use age, rather than mileage, to determine the need to replace a vehicle—that might be at age 15 up to age 20, depending on the car.

Financially, it makes more sense to maintain your car properly than to buy a new one just because the mileage is climbing. I advise my customers to take care of their cars in other ways, as well. Take care of the exterior. These harsh winters are tough on them. Also, you'll want to thoroughly detail the interior, as well, on at least an annual basis. With the accumulation of dust, pollen, animal hair, dander and dirt, the interior of your car can affect your health—especially if you have allergies.

www.AAtheShop.com

CAR CARE 101

Communication can easily break down in my industry due to the many acronyms we use. Listed here are some of the most common ones. I hope these will help you make informed decisions about keeping your vehicle serviced properly.

LOF = Lube, Oil and Filter Service

LOF is pronounced "loaf." What's a "loaf?" In our industry, 'LOF' means Lube, Oil and Filter. Interestingly enough, not a lot of cars receive lubrication anymore, but the acronym has carried over for many years. So, if you see the term "LOF," that refers to an oil change on a vehicle.

ABS = Anti-Lock Brake System

If you read that as a word, it says "abs." So, if we were a gym, you would think of something totally different—one part of your body. But in the car industry, ABS is an acronym for Anti-lock Brake System. So, if your "ABS" light comes on, that means there's a fault in the Anti-lock Brake System. (As far as your body is concerned, check with the gym on that!)

DIS = Driver Information System

This is the vehicle's system that gives the driver information—in an LED-type style, or scrolling across the dash or touch screen, or perhaps visible in a small window somewhere on the dash. Pay close attention to any message and look for specific responses in the index of your owner's manual.

CSS = Cooling System Service

CSS is our acronym for Cooling System Service. That's the process where we typically drain your cooling system and reinstall coolant. It's not a chemical flush; it's just a simple service of your cooling system fluid.

ASE = Automotive Service Excellence

You'll see this one a lot. ASE is an independent organization that tests the competency of those in our industry. ASE does not do training; they only do testing for competency. The training takes place in another location or through other venues, much like a student taking the SAT exam. It's administered at a testing location with a proctor and the results are provided by the certifying organization.

ASE says, "We're going to see if you learned anything through what you have studied. And if you can pass our test, then we will certify that you know what you are talking about and are qualified to repair these specific systems." When someone passes their exam, they become "ASE Certified," and for the automotive repair side of our industry, there are eight different areas of ASE certification. If you are certified in all eight, you are an ASE Master Technician.

ASE also has specific certifications for diesel trucks. They have certifications for light-duty and heavy-duty diesel trucks, certifications for people working in a parts department and certifications for service advisors.

ASE is the "gold standard" in our industry, and in my opinion, it is critical that anyone who works on your vehicle should be an ASE Certified technician. Before you have any work done on your vehicle, ask if the technician assigned to your car is ASE Certified. If they aren't, you may want to look for a repair shop with fully trained and certified technicians and service advisors.

An ASE Certification has to be renewed every five years. This is important because cars and technology change. Therefore, ASE Certified Technicians must stay up to date on cutting-edge technology so they can continue to service your vehicles properly. Every year there are over a million pages of new information hitting our industry, so it's important for my staff and me to stay current.

Your great-grandfather may have said all he needed to fix his car was a piece of bailing wire, a pair of pliers and some duct tape. That may have been true back then, but today, we need a little more than that. That is why being ASE Certified is so important.

TPMS = Tire Pressure Monitoring System

TPMS stands for Tire Pressure Monitoring System. Like the name says, this system monitors the tire pressure of your car. After Ford had problems with accidents caused by low air pressure on their vehicles' tires, the federal government mandated that all vehicles, beginning in 2008-2009, must contain a Tire Pressure Monitoring System. Subaru began implementing them in some models as early as 2006.

Today, the technology actually notifies the driver when a tire has low pressure. Some systems will tell you about a specific tire—for instance, "your left front tire is low." Some simply indicate that you have a low tire somewhere on the vehicle. Spare tires also have these sensors—so although the four tires on the ground may be fine, you should still check the spare tire, as well.

EGR = Exhaust Gas Recirculation

EGR is an acronym you'll hear often. It stands for Exhaust Gas Recirculation. It is an emission control item and a system that recirculates exhaust gases back into the engine for re-burning. Also, fumes from your gas tank return to the engine for re-burning through this system. This has to do with fuel economy and proper engine operation.

TPS = Throttle Position Sensor

In the past, a car had a physical cable that connected the gas pedal with the throttle control mechanism on the engine. Today, instead of a cable, your vehicle uses a throttle position sensor, which means that your actual gas pedal is now a sensor itself. So, when you push down on the gas pedal, you are moving a sensor. The gas pedal sensor information is sent to the throttle position sensors, which tell the onboard computer how much gas and air to allow into the engine.

PCM = Powertrain Control Module

The PCM is the grandfather of the computer systems on the vehicle. It is the mission control center, the head honcho, the king, the president—it is what everything else goes through. Typically, there are many computers within a single car; and they all communicate with the PCM.

BCM = Body Control Module

The Body Control Module pays attention to everything internal (inside the vehicle). "Things you touch" is a simple way to define what goes through the BCM—for example, turn signals, headlights, heating and air controls and other items like these. They all send information through the Body Control Module.

AT = Automatic Transmission

This is the type of transmission most passenger vehicles have. In fact, it's increasingly difficult to find a standard transmission anymore. If your gearshift has choices like "Park," "Reverse" and "Drive," you have an automatic transmission. This type of transmission automatically shifts when certain conditions exist.

The invention of the automatic transmission revolutionized the driving of vehicles. Before this time, the driver had to manually shift their car into different gears. That's why it's called a "manual" or standard transmission.

Dashboard = Lights that pop up on the dashboard

As you sit in the driver's seat and turn on the key, you see various lights pop up on the dashboard. But what do they mean?

First, there's a reason for the color of lights on your dashboard. These colors can be associated with the traffic lights you see when you are driving down the road.

If you see a RED light, what does that usually mean to you? Stop. And when you see YELLOW? Caution. GREEN? Green means go.

So let's apply this to the dashboard lights. If, for example, you have the cruise control on, the button is normally some sort of orange color. Once you set the cruise control, the button turns green.

Dashboard lights are very important and should never be ignored. If one of your orange or red dashboard lights comes on, you need to have your vehicle serviced by a qualified technician.

ABS Light:

The ABS light has to do with the brakes, as we mentioned previously. If the ABS light is on, the Anti-lock Brake System computer has found a fault somewhere in the system. It could be anything from low brake fluid to a problem with a particular wheel sensor or another component within the system.

When the ABS light is on, your normal braking will still work. However, if you get into a panic stop, the anti-lock brake system will *not* take over your braking—that is, your wheels will lock up like a vehicle not equipped with anti-lock brakes. Therefore, you lose the ability to maneuver around objects in your path. Instead, momentum carries you forward, and you'll likely hit the object ahead of you.

You may remember your parents telling you that if you're on ice you should pump your brakes and not apply them hard. The ABS System uses that principle, as well.

The ABS system pumps your brakes ten times per second, which is something no human is able to do.

The ABS light typically comes on as a red light in most vehicles. In a Subaru, it is typically an orange light. It doesn't mean that you have to immediately stop the car, but it does indicate that the system is not going to work until you get it resolved. It does not mean that your car won't stop; it does not mean that your brakes have failed completely; it only means that the anti-lock side of your brake system is not going to operate if you get into a panic stop situation or trying to stop on a slick surface. Drive cautiously—as you always should—and quickly get your vehicle to a shop for testing.

Check Engine Light:

The check engine light has been around since about 1990. Its initial purpose was to provide information about the emission control status of the vehicle. Check engine lights are typically orange in color because they still primarily deal with emission controls. However, emission controls now includes additional elements, as well.

Emissions concerns air pollution—so, for instance, if a spark plug is not working properly, it causes the car to pollute more than it should, and the check engine light comes on.

Formerly, a failed spark plug wouldn't cause the check engine light to come on. It would come on if you had a fuel canister that was full of gasoline or if the EGR (Exhaust Gas Recirculation, remember) system failed. Now, the check engine light encompasses many things; there are somewhere between six hundred and nine hundred different reasons why the check engine light might come on. A technician needs to run tests on the system to determine the actual cause so they can correct this problem.

SRS Light:

Air bags are very important. In a car equipped with air bags you will see an SRS light (or Air Bag light) on the dashboard. SRS is an acronym for Supplementary Restraint System—the key word being *supplementary*.

That means it supplements your safety system, and that safety system is your seat belt. If you are not wearing your seat belt when you are in an accident that deploys the airbags, a greater amount of bodily injury will occur. For that reason, *you should ALWAYS wear your seatbelt.*

If the airbag light is on, there is a problem in the system and the airbags will not deploy if an accident occurs. As you can imagine, this can be very serious. If your SRS light comes on, get your vehicle to the shop quickly.

Traction Control Light:

The vehicle computer not only monitors the brake system and airbags, but it also helps move power from one tire to another in all-wheel-drive vehicles. For example, in an all-wheel drive vehicle, let's say you become stuck on ice or in snow and are trying to get out. One of your wheels is usually stuck worse than the others—it's spinning but not getting any traction. The traction control system will move the power from the wheel that is spinning to a wheel that is not, since the non-spinning wheel has greater traction. The traction control system allows power to be transferred so that you can gain traction, have greater control and get out of a situation where you may normally remain stuck.

Traction control also works during acceleration. An example of acceleration mode is when you turn a corner and the weight of the car shifts from one side to the other.

The traction control system is going to move the power to the wheels with the best traction.

The traction control light comes on momentarily whenever the system activates. If there's a failure in the system, the light will stay on. That is when you need to take your vehicle for inspection.

Reduced Power Light:

Reduced power is something primarily seen on GM vehicles. The reduced power light is usually red and indicates that something has gone wrong, that the vehicle has gone into "limp mode"—as in "we are limping" or "we only have one leg and cannot run." Such a fault in this system could be problematic. Many times, this fault pertains to either transmission functions or accelerating functions. If this light comes on, you must get it in for service.

Some limp modes limit your speed to no more than 25 miles an hour, which will allow you to drive to a safe place. You'll likely need to have it towed from that point, especially if you have a long way to go. Other limp modes allow you to go 40 miles per hour, usually enough that you can get to a repair facility on your own.

The reduced power light will most always be red. It indicates a problem that needs to receive immediate attention.

Temperature Light:

Most cars today have an engine temperature gauge as well as a temperature light. The engine temperature light will always be red, indicating that you need to shut the car down as soon as possible. The longer you continue to drive, the more damage will occur. Eventually, you will damage the engine internally. By continuing to drive the vehicle, you will create more problems—very costly problems.

When the temperature light comes on, you should pull over, look at the temperature gauge, and if it's too hot, turn the engine off as quickly as you safely can. The first step in the troubleshooting process is to make sure that your coolant level is full.

But be careful! You have to use extreme caution when adding coolant to a car that is hot because you can be burned. It is best to let the car sit for several hours to cool down before adding coolant.

The need to add coolant indicates you have a leak that needs to be repaired. If the coolant is full and the vehicle is running hot, that means that a component within the system has failed. Either way, you'll need to get your car to the shop quickly.

Oil Light:

The oil light can indicate an issue with the oil level or oil pressure—sometimes both. If the engine loses oil pressure, the oil light is going to come on. That light will be red because you have to shut the engine down quickly. If the oil pressure is too low, there will be internal damage to the engine. The damage would be similar to driving without oil in the engine.

To clarify, you can be low on oil and still have oil pressure. The oil light may not let you know that you are low on oil—in some cars, only checking the level with a dipstick can tell you if you are low on oil. (One new technology in some of the higher end cars, like BMW and Mercedes models uses no dipstick. Instead, there is a sensor inside the engine that reads the oil level and indicates its level. Most cars still have a dipstick.)

Even when you're a quart or two low on oil, you still have enough oil in the engine to produce oil pressure. In that case, the oil light might not come on because adequate oil pressure exists. But the lower your oil level, the more stress and damage to your engine occurs.

Potentially, you could have a low oil level and no indicator light to warn you. That's why regular oil changes are so important.

Having a sufficient oil level provides several benefits. Lubricating the engine is the oil's primary job, but it also increases fuel mileage.

Smart Air Bag Light:

Almost all cars are equipped with smart air bags. These sensors measure the weight of the person in the front passenger seat. Depending on the weight of the person or object in that seat, the air bag may or may not deploy. With this light, there is nothing you need to do. If there is a small child in the front seat, the smart bag knows it. If the weight in the front seat does not meet a certain criterion established by the manufacturer, the smart air bag light will come on to let you know that the airbag is off on the passenger side.

The reason the airbag doesn't deploy with a child in the front passenger seat is because the car industry has learned that small children cannot withstand the explosion of an airbag.

The inside of an airbag contains a substance similar to gunpowder. When triggered, the "gunpowder" explodes the bag out of the dash at an extremely high rate of speed. The air inside that bag immediately deflates, but is present for just long enough to provide a cushion to the blow of an impact.

Typically, the occupant of the seat moves forward while the bag deploys rearward, so a collision takes place between the bag and the occupant. Because the airbag deploys at such a high rate of speed, a child's body simply cannot withstand that kind of force and injury or death can occur. After learning this, car manufacturers introduced smart bags—which was quite a "smart" thing to do.

Many cars have not only dashboard lights but also dashboard gauges. The following are the primary gauges you'll find on the dashboard of vehicles today. They allow us a quick and easy way to tell how well our car is functioning.

Temperature Gauge:

One common gauge is the cold/hot gauge, also called the coolant

temperature gauge. Typically, you will find the coolant temperature gauge on the left side of the dash. This gauge, mentioned previously, monitors the temperature of the engine.

Transmissions usually will not shift into the final drive gear until the engine temperature has reached at least a quarter of the way of its full gauge range. Most gauges are set to run—in normal operation—about midway up the gauge. So, you'll usually see a "C" (for cold) on the bottom and an "H" (for hot) on the top (or Blue for cold and Red for hot).

The gauge could also be horizontally installed—in that case, the 'C' would be on the left and the 'H' would be on the right. The needle is typically going to be in the middle of the gauge, indicating what is called, "Operating Temperature."

Interestingly, if the indicator needle indicates your engine is staying cold, that impacts your fuel mileage. The vehicle's computer is designed to put fuel in the engine based on a certain engine temperature. When the engine is cold, it puts in more fuel because a cold engine needs more. If the thermostat is not working—the typical failure—then the computer perceives that the engine is running at a colder temperature and continues putting more fuel into the engine. Thus, you will use more gasoline. Therefore, because the thermostat can impact fuel mileage, it is important that you are familiar with the temperature gauge to know what is normal. It is all about checking that gauge on a consistent basis. Remember: If you continue to run the vehicle when the gauge shows the engine is hot, this will cause expensive and critical internal engine damage.

Tachometer:

Most tachometer gauges (also called "tachs"

or RPM gauges) are circular and have a series of numbers on them—often 0-8.

Even if you are sitting still, you will see the tachometer needle move around the gauge as you accelerate by pressing on the gas pedal. The tachometer indicates how many times the engine is rotating each minute. Multiply the number on the gauge by one thousand—for example, if the needle is sitting at 1, the engine is rotating one thousand times per minute. (If the numbers on the tachometer are multiples of 10—numbers like 20, 30, 40, and so on—then you multiply that number by one hundred instead of one thousand.) That number is how many times the engine makes one full revolution each minute—called revolutions per minute or "RPMs" for short.

It can be helpful to keep an eye on the RPM gauge. The RPM number will drop each time the transmission shifts into a higher gear to increase fuel economy. If you notice that the engine appears to be running at a higher

RPM than normal, it may indicate that something is not right—that the engine is working harder than usual.

Another situation when the tachometer is helpful is as you are idling. If you have a vacuum leak or a similar problem, your idling RPM will be higher than usual. Most engines should run just below the 1 mark. If the idling RPM is significantly higher, that's a problem. You should expect to see the idling RPM a little bit higher when the engine is cold. Once the engine reaches operating temperature, you will see the gauge go back down to the 650-750 RPM range. Isn't understanding acronyms cool?

Battery Gauge:

The battery gauge simply measures battery voltage. You will usually see a small picture of a battery. It indicates battery problems. Some gauges will have a number 12, which concerns the voltage, but most of the time the normal position for the needle, when everything is fine with the battery, is in the middle of the gauge.

Fuel Gauge:

Most people know that "E" does not stand for "enough"—it stands for empty. And "F" of course stands for full.

In today's cars, the fuel pump is located *inside* the gas tank. Having enough fuel in the tank helps keep that little electric motor—called your fuel pump—cool, and will typically make it last longer.

As a general rule, you should keep at least a quarter tank of fuel in your car at all times. This will add life to the fuel pump because, since it is an electric motor, it does create heat, and excessive heat shortens the life of the pump. That's why keeping enough fuel in the tank helps it last longer.

My advice is to completely refuel your car when your gauge indicates a quarter of a tank. If you always running that quarter to empty range, you're going to shorten the life of the pump. Not only that, but when you need to get somewhere right away, you will want more than a quarter of a tank of gas.

Odometer:

The odometer gauge tells you how many miles are on your vehicle. The accuracy of an odometer gauge has changed over the years. Today it's electronic, whereas years ago, a cable ran from the speedometer head down to the transmission. As the transmission rotated, this cable rotated. Because of that, odometer readings could be altered. That's impossible with the LED-displayed odometers we have today. The odometer gauge accurately shows how many miles are on a car.

Speedometer:

The speedometer gauge is, of course, useful for showing how fast you are moving. Its speed sensors are reliable and accurate. This information tells the transmission when to shift.

Noises

One of the greatest things about car ownership is really getting to know your car. That means using your five senses—hearing, sight, smell, taste, and touch. You can use your senses to know what is normal for *your* car so you'll recognize when something has changed.

When it comes to hearing noises that you know are not normal—not what you are used to hearing—one of the best things to do is "show the noise."

When you take the car into a service facility, don't try to explain the noise. *Show* them the noise. One of the greatest helps to any service facility is when the vehicle owner pays attention so they can duplicate the noise.

- How fast was I going?

- Was I turning?

- Was I braking?

- Was I accelerating?

- What were the scenarios?

- Was I going uphill or downhill?

Pay attention to the environment and the activity that is taking place when the noise occurs. Then you can take that information, go to the repair facility, get someone in the car with you and duplicate the sound. Highly trained automotive technicians can typically hear many noises that you may not hear. This small step will assist the technician in locating and correcting the same noise that concerned you. When you pay attention to how the car normally sounds, you'll recognize when something changes.

Brake Squeaking

One common noise that often scares people is a squeaky noise that happens when you push on your brake pedal. A high-pitched noise is indicative of brakes needing repair, especially if this is a new sound. Sometimes what we'll call "inferior" brake pads or "inferior" parts can be used on a brake job. In those cases, you should expect some squeaking.

The sound is not necessarily metal contacting metal, but actually a vibration of the brake pad against the rotor, which comes out as an audible squeak. The vibration is at a decibel level that sounds like a squeak, so this can occur due to the type of brake pad used or the surface of the rotor.

However, if you have a good brake system and use high quality parts, you should not hear any noise. If noise occurs at some point in the future, you should recognize it as a problem and have the brake system inspected for any wear, tear, or other issue.

Brake Grinding

Grinding usually happens after squeaking. Some brakes never squeak, but go straight to grinding. That is typically metal grinding on metal, and you definitely need to get your vehicle into a shop.

Some of the higher end manufacturers, such as Mercedes, BMW and Lexus, have what are called "brake pad wear indicators." These are just small wires built into the brake pad. Once that wire makes contact with the rotor, a dash light comes on that says "brake wear indicator." At that point, you can bet it is time to replace your pads. Once the sensor makes contact with the rotor, the sensor is ruined and will have to be replaced along with the brake pads.

Squeaky Engine

Many times, you'll find a plastic splash shield installed underneath the front of the car for multiple purposes. They not only prevent foreign objects from getting into the engine compartment and causing damage, but also protect against water getting into the drive belt area. If water enters that area, the drive belt may actually slip on the pulleys. You are hearing the squeaking noise because water intrusion has occurred. This is not especially harmful but it probably means that the shield is either disfigured or not there at all.

Shields are frequently damaged when you pull too close to parking spots and hit the sidewalk curb slightly, or when you hit one of those parking stops because your car sits a little bit lower than the average vehicle. If you hit the shield enough times, eventually it will come off.

If that happens, your lower engine area will be exposed and could sustain damage from water, a rock, or other debris. Check to see if this plastic shield is in good condition when you wash your car or get fuel. It only takes a moment, and could save you thousands of dollars in repairs.

Thumping While Turning

Sometimes when you turn, you will hear a thumping noise and possibly feel a jerking action through the steering wheel. Several problems could cause this thumping noise.

One problem could be your "constant velocity joints" (or CV joints). Your axle has a constant velocity joint built into it that maintains quickness of motion to the wheels when you turn your steering wheel. When CV joints wear out, they cause a thumping or knocking noise when you turn. The only repair option is to replace the axle itself.

Another thumping noise involves the brakes. Usually occurring at highway speeds, you will hearth is when you apply the brakes. It could be something you hear or something you feel. Many times, you see the steering wheel shake.

That usually means the rotors, which are a brake component, are out of round. Those rotors turn with the wheel as you drive. When you apply the brakes, the brake pads rub against the rotor to create the friction that causes your vehicle to slow down. If the surface of the rotor is not smooth or straight, it produces a thumping noise or a vibration.

Another phrase we hear is described as a "pulsation of the brakes" when they're applied. You typically hear or feel that pulsation when you brake at speeds above 45 miles per hour. You may not necessarily feel the pulsations if you are braking at 20 miles per hour, but once you get up to highway speeds and apply the brakes, you are more likely to feel or hear the vibrations.

Though not necessarily a dangerous situation, it can be quite a nuisance. It also has a negative impact on brake pad and suspension life.

Thumping While Driving

If you hear a regular thumping or vibration that varies with your speed as you're driving down the road, the tires are usually the culprit. Many times, the tread in the tire is separating internally.

Want a sure-fire way to know if this has occurred? Try this: Drive across a parking lot at 2 to 3 miles per hour, then let go of the steering wheel. If your steering wheel shakes back and forth, slightly left to right, that's an indication that the tread has moved inside the tire, and you definitely need to replace the tires.

The age at which you should replace a tire has become an issue over the years. All tires have a number on them that indicates the age of the tire. The number will start with the letters DOT (an abbreviation for Department of Transportation), followed by a series of letters and numbers. At the end of the series will be four digits. Those digits represent the week and year the tire was made. For instance, if one of your tires has the digits 4512, the tire was made in the 45th week of 2012. The numerical significance comes into play because the recommendation for replacing tires is between five and seven years old.

Check your tires. If they are 10 years old, they definitely need to be replaced. If you don't replace them, you are at a great risk of a blow out or tire separation.

Whining Engine

Whining usually occurs either from the children in the back seat or from the car's steering pump under the hood. You'll want to check both of those possibilities. You may need a cookie for one and power steering fluid for the other.

The power steering fluid is a sealed system for the most part. If you need to add power steering fluid, you most likely have a leak somewhere in the system. Adding fluid will be a temporary measure. If you have a leak, the whine may stop for a while, but once the fluid leaks out again, the whining noise will resume. Take your car for servicing if you suspect a power steering fluid leak.

Vehicle Starting

When you start your car, several noises may be heard. One is a tapping noise that can indicate that your oil is not getting where it needs to be. That noise occurs because some areas of the car need to have oil immediately upon starting. One reason some of the manufacturers have gone to a lighter weight oil is because it can get to those areas that need lubrication quicker on start-up.

Another noise you might hear is a rattling. Any time you hear a rattle in your engine when you start your car, it is metal-to-metal contact. While it will not cause *immediate* failure, problems will happen eventually. The cause is usually a low oil level, low oil pressure, or it could signal that internal wear has occurred.

On some of the Subaru engines, there is a piston knock. This is not uncommon and relatively harmless, in most cases. A trained technician can easily determine this for you. The pistons have been redesigned on the later models to alleviate this issue.

CAR CARE 201

In this section, let's explore some of the more advanced areas of your vehicle, including when to buy a new one. This could become a reference manual for you and a great training manual for new drivers in your family. I've structured this section in the form of a Question and Answer series, much like an FAQ section of a website or resource book.

Buying a New Car

Let's discuss a few of the most frequently questions related to purchasing a new vehicle. Having this information could save you thousands of dollars.

Q. When do I need to buy a new car versus investing in the one I have?

A. Every car has a point of diminishing return. What you do from the day you drive your car off the showroom floor and whether you think of your vehicle as an investment or as an expense affects the decisions you make about replacing it.

You should not say, "Well, I don't want to put that much money into my car." If you've maintained the car well, you should expect to get 300,000 to 400,000 miles from it. When you buy a vehicle, you have to understand that how you maintain it today is going to determine its condition tomorrow. With proper servicing, your point of diminishing returns is going to be a lot farther down the road than if you neglect it.

I have seen vehicles with as few as 75,000 miles need an engine (between $5,500 and $6,800) simply because the oil was not changed properly.

It is always better to maintain a car correctly from the beginning so that the point of diminishing returns is much farther out than it otherwise would be.

Let's say you have a six or seven-year-old vehicle. Perhaps it needs a timing belt, or has blown a head gasket. It is going to cost $2,500 to $3,500 to repair a vehicle you have been driving for six to seven years. You are just not sure you want to pay that much to get it fixed, so you consider buying a new car. Here's a calculation that may help you decide.

Larry Burkett was a well-known financial advisor who started Crown Financial Ministries. He would tell you that the cheapest car you will ever own is the one in your driveway. What he means is that by having the car maintained and having everything in good working order, you will spend less money than purchasing a newer vehicle.

When we talk about making a major repair on a car, a way you can try to crunch the numbers is to ask yourself, "What's it going to cost me over the next year?"

Let's say there is $3,000 worth of work that needs to be done on your vehicle and you have decided you are not going to repair it. Instead, you are going to go buy a used vehicle. Even if you bought an inexpensive one, around $10,000, there's still the down payment, then the calculated monthly payments if you finance. Of course, depending on the state, you might also have to pay sales tax on that vehicle. Plus, you'll need to figure an almost immediate depreciation, as well. Your personal property taxes will go up. Your insurance will increase because, if you finance the car, you'll have to have full coverage insurance. Calculate your total cost over the next 12 months for that used car and compare that to the cost of making repairs on the one in your driveway.

If you apply this same principle to buying a brand new car, these dollar figures are going to go up exponentially. Therefore, it almost always makes more sense to fix your existing car than to buy a new one.

Extended Warranties

Q: If I buy a new vehicle, should I purchase an extended warranty?

*A:*I advise my customers not to purchase extended warranties. Evidence proves that, in most cases, the cost of the warranty is far more than the benefit received. (If you're interested in learning more about this, see the appendices in the back of the book.)

Caring for your Car

Q. When should I jump-start my car?

A. The purpose of a battery is to send power to the starter, which then starts the engine. If a problem with the battery exists, it will show up when you try to start the car, not while you're driving.

We've all experienced a dead battery, haven't we? We turn the key and either hear nothing or series of repetitive clicks. The engine does not turn over. That is the only time you should jump-start your car.

If you're driving down the road and your car dies, the battery is not the cause of your car dying. Do not jump-start your car in this situation. It will not help.

Note: *See the "How-To" Section to learn the proper way to jump-start your car.*

Premium Fuel

Q. Do I need to buy premium fuel?

A. The best way to determine if premium fuel is right for you is to consult your owner's manual to see what they recommend for your specific car. Higher-end models will require premium gas. Those cars are designed to burn fuel at optimum levels. Both the way the engine is timed and tuned, and the type of spark plugs used ensures that when you use this fuel, you'll get the optimum performance from your vehicle.

There is nothing wrong with using 87% octane. The engine will automatically change the timing on that vehicle for that particular gasoline.

Components called "knock sensors" were added to vehicles a few years ago. These sensors adjust the timing if the engine begins to "ping" or "knock" as a result of lower octane or other factors in the fuel.

So do you have to use premium fuel? The answer is no. However, if you want the best performance and the best fuel mileage for your particular vehicle, then I would recommend using the higher-grade gasoline.

The return on investment is simply a crunching of the numbers. (Keep in mind that other factors affect gas mileage, as well—how fast we drive, driving conditions, tires, environmental factors, and more.)

If you want to see if you really get better performance, do your own test. Calculate and record your fuel mileage after two or three fill-ups with premium gas. Do the same after two to three fill-ups with lower octane fuel. You should be able to determine if using premium gas makes a difference.

Motor Club Memberships

Q. How beneficial are motor club memberships?

A. Motor clubs provide good benefits for the consumer, and offer peace of mind for the consumer who travels a lot. Undoubtedly, their primary focus is the customer. I am thinking of clubs like AAA Motor Club or Cross Country Motor Club, the two big wheels in the industry. It's easy to feel vulnerable when traveling through an unfamiliar part of the country. These clubs help locate a reliable repair facility, a towing company, a hotel, and other things of that nature. Therefore, you have more confidence in the quality of service you will receive.

However, if you're not a big traveler, most independent repair facilities have a free roadside assistance package for customers who regularly utilize them for basic services.

Introduction to Maintenance

What do we mean when we say, "maintenance?" It's a term which applies to any number of industries and essentially means the same thing in each—it means *care* or *upkeep*.

We've already discussed crucial factors in the care and upkeep of your vehicle—things like engine oils, the benefits of regular services, and so on. Let's address a few other important components of your car's maintenance.

Engine Oil

Here are some common questions about engine oil:

• *Does the type of engine oil I put in really matter?*

• *Can I change the brand of oil I use?*

• *What do the numbers mean?*

All oil today is called "paraffin-based oil." That means the oil has the ability to capture dirt—this is one of its jobs. When an oil  change is performed, we drain the oil from the vehicle and dirt goes with it.

Manufacturers have made changes to the oil for use in lubricating their specific engines. The car industry used to recommend oil based on geographic conditions. If you lived in a cold climate, like Alaska, thinner winter oil would be recommended. If you lived in the warmer southern states, heavier oil might be recommended.

All that has changed due to the tolerances built into cars by the manufacturers. Today it is more important than ever that you pay attention to the type of oil the manufacturer recommends.

The label on a bottle of oil provides information about that oil. Most people examine the weight of the oil first. Is it 5W30? 10W30? What does that even mean? Well, the "W" stands for winter. If we used 5W30 for example, the "5" and "30" actually measure the thickness of the oil at different temperatures.

If an oil bottle has "5W30" on it, in winter climates the oil has a viscosity of 30. Once the oil is heated, it has a viscosity of 5.

Most cars today use either 5W20 or 5W30, regardless of geographic location. The brand you choose is up to you. Contrary to what your grandfather told you it's okay to switch brands.

Oil Change Frequency

How often you should change your oil is becoming an issue in our industry because of changes in service intervals. Years ago, it was every three months or three thousand miles. Our fathers, grandfathers, and great-grandfathers all taught us that. The reason the oil needed changing so often was because the engines were exposed to the elements, and the filtering system of air and fuel was not what it is today. Your oil could be easily contaminated and cause internal engine damage. That is why car engines used to last only about fifty thousand miles.

Several things have changed since then. With the advent of electronic fuel injection, we do not have as much problem with outside elements getting to the crankcase, because the fuel systems are sealed. Fuel is also managed better, so the oil is not contaminated with fuel the way it used to.

Thus, we have better control of outside elements, like dirt and dust, coming into the engine, and we have better control through better filtering. We have more control of the amount of fuel that is dumped into an engine for burning—almost all of it is being burned these days.

The last element is that oil has gotten better at suspending dirt and particulates in the engine. Using this argument, the "oil experts" and manufacturers conclude that you can go up to 7,500 miles or more between oil and filter changes.

What they fail to tell you is that the cylinder compression in modern engines has doubled and with this increased engine performance comes blow-by of oil past the piston rings, and oil is burned in the combustion process. This also develops sludge, which causes the rings to stick. Simply put, we burn more oil. Add into this factor an extreme environment with a wide temperature variant, like Alaska, or the other mountain states and oil change intervals become more critical.

For instance, when I start my Subaru in the winter at -10F and inspect the tail pipe, I smell gas. This is perfectly normal because the temperature sensor is telling the computer to send more fuel to the injectors to keep the car running—exactly how the mechanical choke on Dad's car worked all those years ago. What happens, though, is more gas gets into the crankcase and dilutes the oil, thinning it and multiplying the "blow-by," increasing the oil consumption. Multiply this times cold morning and evening startups times five working days a week and you start to get accelerated wear due to low and diluted oil.

To further complicate this, on many other cars there are life monitors that tell you when it's time to change your oil. So you have to be aware of when you want to change your oil and adhere to those mileage intervals.

My personal opinion is that, in extreme environmental conditions, your oil should be changed every 3,000 miles or 3 months. I maintain the same opinion on non-extreme geographical areas simply because it is the best and least expensive maintenance item that you can do for the longevity of your car. If you decided to go through the extended mileage exercise, make sure you have extra oil and add it, because you will need it. The other primary reason to do this is because you have professional technicians inspecting your vehicle, in most cases at no charge, to make sure you have no driving issues and, let me tell you, that's peace of mind in the cold, dark, Alaskan winter.

Transmission Fluid

In the section on motor oil, we covered the fact that dirt is suspended in the oil. At each oil change, the oil (and the dirt it holds) drains out of your car and clean oil is added. Can we apply the same reasoning with transmissions?

Transmissions don't pull in air, but they do have metal-to-metal contact, or the potential for metal-to-metal contact (this is true with every component on your car where fluids are involved). Transmissions are also exposed to heat.

Heat, plus metal-to-metal contact eventually breaks down the fluid which circulates through the system. The good news is that we do not have to service the transmission every 3,000 miles. In extreme service areas, it is good to follow the manufacturer's recommendations. In this case, it's every 30,000 miles. If you use your Subaru to tow or do more winter four-wheeling, you may consider doing them more often. The good news is that Subaru makes an awesome all-wheel-drive transmission.

Differential Fluid

We can apply this same concept to the differential. On most front-wheel-drive vehicles, the differential is a part of the transmission. The differential on rear-wheel-drive cars is located in another part of the transmission. Differentials also need occasional fluid changes.

Power Steering Fluid

These same principles and guidelines apply to the power steering system. This system is predominantly a "closed" or "sealed" system, but over time, this fluid needs to be changed to protect the components from wearing from the inside. Remember, it is always less expensive to change the fluid that protects the part than to replace the part itself.

Brake Fluid

Unlike the previous aspects of maintenance, brake fluid is not added at particular intervals. Instead, we can measure when brake fluid or coolant should be changed. The measurement for when brake fluid should be flushed is 200 copper parts per million.

Brake fluid is hydroscopic, which means that if you left the can open overnight, the contents would be ruined because the moisture it would absorb overnight would render it unusable inside your vehicle. It is *imperative* to keep brake fluid tightly sealed.

Brake fluid is designed to absorb moisture in your brake system since moisture deteriorates all the metal components the brake fluid comes in contact with. Brake fluid is a hydraulic fluid crucial to proper braking.

If your brake fluid becomes too heated (especially heated to boiling) it creates air bubbles. If you've ever had air in your system, you know that the brake pedal goes to the floor and still doesn't stop the car! It's a horrifying experience.

Once the fluid reaches 200 copper parts per million, the brake fluid's boiling point is reduced, which could potentially cause problems. The destruction to your brakes would not occur suddenly, so by the time it causes actual problems, your system could already be ruined—which will be quite an expensive repair.

Since we have started doing brake flushes on vehicles, we seldom have to replace the calipers. Many chain stores will put new calipers on your car as part of a routine brake job, but they typically are not needed.

Most brake flushes currently cost less than $100, and need to be done every two to four years (depending on fluid measurements and the environment), whereas brake caliper replacements will cost between $500 and $600.

That's another important reason you should take your car to a licensed technician who will keep it in proper running condition and replace fluids appropriately. The old Ben Franklin quote about an ounce of prevention being worth more than a pound of cure is really true when it comes to maintenance on your car.

Cooling System

The cooling system's primary component is antifreeze/coolant, which helps keep the engine from freezing in the winter, and keeps it cool in the summer. As with brake fluid, a measurement can be made to determine when your coolant needs to be replaced.

In this case, we measure the pH level, which is an indicator of the acidic protection that the fluid is capable of providing, and the freeze point. For instance, a pH level of 7.0 is neutral, indicating that the coolant is no longer protecting the soft metals inside your engine. It's like having straight water in your cooling system, which is detrimental because it deteriorates the metal inside the system. This shortens the life of your heater core, radiator, and cylinder heads.

The cooling system should be measured at 10,000-mile intervals. Usually a cooling system repair will cost $500 to $1,000. In contrast, having the coolant flushed costs less than $100. You are saving long-term dollars by maintaining your vehicle on a regular basis.

Air Conditioning

In states with sweltering hot summers, few things are more frustrating than having your air conditioning blow hot air when it is over 100° outside. Your air conditioning system is a sealed system.

We know from previous discussions that in a closed system the only way you will suffer a loss in fluid or, in this case, refrigerant, is for you to have a leak in the system. Having the air conditioning evacuated and recharged about every three to five years is a good maintenance guideline.

The A/C system uses oil, which is carried throughout the system by the refrigerant. If you have a leak in the system, the oil will be too low to protect those expensive A/C components. Just like running your engine without oil, running your A/C system without oil will damage your A/C "engine," (also known as the compressor).

Some compressors look like very small engines on the inside. They have some of the same components as your car's engine—pistons, rings, rods and a crank shaft, only much smaller. Keeping the compressor well-lubricated extends its longevity.

You should ALWAYS have your A/C system serviced by an ASE Certified Technician. It's just too dangerous to do yourself.

> **NEVER** attempt to recharge your air conditioning system yourself!

Keeping your air conditioning system serviced every couple of years is a great way to save money and stay cool in the heat of summer.

Years ago, a technician might spend five minutes diagnosing a car and five hours making the repair. Today, we might spend five hours running tests and diagnosing the vehicle, and five minutes repairing or putting a component on it. The cost of electronics drives this change.

Vehicles today have a tremendous number of electronic systems. It is not unusual to find between five and fifteen computers on any given car. It is imperative that all those computers communicate with each other. And the main computer is the Power Train Control Module. All other computers must communicate with this "mission control center" through a CAN—Controlled Area Network. Investigating these various computer systems can become complex.

Again, this is where experienced, certified technicians are worth their weight in gold. Let the professionals do their jobs—taking care of the upkeep for your car.

CAR CARE 301– "How To"

No book like this would be complete without a "How To" section. There are many things on a car that you can do yourself, and in this section, I want to discuss the proper way to do them.

How to Change a Flat Tire

Most vehicles have a tire pressure monitoring system that will indicate that you have a low tire. Technology has increased to the point that some cars even tell you which tire is low, so pay attention to your dash lights. If that light comes on, you need to quickly find a safe place to investigate the situation.

Tires can go flat over a short *or* a long period of time, depending on the size of the hole. When you need to change a tire, *the most dangerous place for you to change it is on the edge of the interstate.* If possible, get off the interstate, even if that means driving on the shoulder at a very slow speed until you can exit—or at least to an area of the road where you can safely pull off the road (which, to me, is at least 15 to 20 feet from the edge of the freeway). Ideally, you want to exit and get to a safe location out of sight of the freeway, where you can raise the car using the tools provided. A lighted area is preferable if this happens at night.

If you've never changed a flat before, let me encourage you to practice doing so in the safety and comfort of your garage or driveway. Become familiar with the tools and the procedure. Follow the directions given in the driver's manual. If you have children of or near driving age, demonstrate the technique to them and then let them duplicate the process. The last thing you want to do is figure out how to change a flat when you're pulled off the side of a road!

The owner's manual will tell you the exact location where you must place the jack in order to raise the vehicle safely. You can cause damage to the car, or become injured, if you place it incorrectly. Here's another little hint: Always loosen (but don't remove) the lug nuts holding the wheel in place *before* you jack up the car. It's much easier to remove the tire if you do it that way.

When putting the spare tire on, be sure to start each of the lug nuts by hand. Remember to put the beveled edge of the lug nut toward the wheel. Then, with your tire iron, tighten them in a star pattern. To do this, tighten one, then skip one, tighten one, then skip one. Eventually, all five nuts will be tight.

Most cars come with the wrench or tire iron you use to tighten the lug nuts. To make it easier to change the tire, position the wrench in such a way that you can stand on it, using your leg and body weight to loosen each lug nut. However, you do not want to do that while tightening the lug nuts (because you can over-tighten them). After tightening all of the lug nuts, drive 50 to 100 miles, then check them again to make sure they are still tight.

How to Jump-Start a Car

Jump-starting a car is actually controlling a spark. You're running an electrical current from one  battery to another. That gives you two batteries with the potential to vent acid gas. Therefore, a controlled spark of electricity reduces the risk of injury and/or damage.

What we mean by "venting" is that it's not uncommon for battery fumes from the acid inside to slowly leak from the top of the battery. Since acid is explosive, you could potentially blow up the battery if you don't control that spark. Moreover, if your face happens to be in the vicinity at the time, bad things could happen. If you have safety glasses, it would be a good idea to wear them when you jump-start a car. Safety glasses are about $3.00 at most places. I keep a pair in my vehicle for just such a situation.

Before doing anything, blow on both batteries before making a connection. An old battery recycler taught me this lesson and it works. It purges the potentially explosive gasses around the battery area and, in case of an accidental spark, the area is less prone to ignite in an explosion.

Here's how to properly jump start a car: With the engine running on the "good battery" car,

1. Connect the jumper cable to the ground (negative terminal) of the "good" battery.
2. Connect the other end of that cable to the ground (negative terminal) of the "bad" battery.
3. Connect the other side of the cable to the positive terminal of the "bad" battery.
4. Connect the final cable to the positive terminal of the "good" battery.
5. Have the driver of the "bad" car start the engine. It should start right up.
6. Carefully remove the cables in reverse order.

Jump-starting a car essentially uses electricity from the good battery to power the bad one, thus making an electrical circuit. Making the last connection to the positive terminal of your good battery will minimize the possibility

of an uncontrolled spark, thus keeping you and your battery

safe.

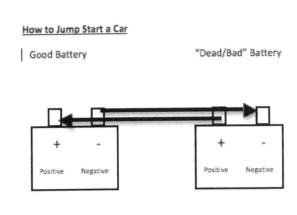

How to Jump Start a Car

Good Battery   "Dead/Bad" Battery

Positive   Negative   Positive   Negative

Connect Negative Good to Negative Bad,

THEN

Connect Positive Bad to Positive Good.

When jump-starting a car, remember: Good, Bad, Bad,

Good.

How to Manage a Breakdown

You should be familiar enough with your gauges to

know what "normal" is, so when the gauges are not within

normal range, you will realize something is wrong.

When you are driving, and begin to feel something about the function of your car that you are unsure about, or hear a new noise, cautiously move into the right lane. You do *not* want your vehicle to be disabled in the left lane or in the median of a freeway. Always try to get to a safe location to manage a breakdown—not only for your sake, but for that of your passengers and your car.

If your vehicle begins to overheat, the gauges will indicate it, so keep an eye on them. If your vehicle *is* overheating, turn the engine off as soon as possible.

The second thing you should do during a breakdown is to make a call. These days most people carry cell phones. I recommend you keep numbers for a towing company, motor club or repair shop in your phone for such an emergency.

Make sure you're in a safe spot and keep passengers a safe distance from the highway as you wait for help to arrive. This will decrease your risk of an accident.

Managing a breakdown, though sometimes nerve-racking and always inconvenient, is not that complicated. Try to remember the following:

1. Don't panic!

2. Think "safety."

3. Call for assistance.

How to Manage an Accident

Having an accident is always an emotional situation—whether that emotion is anger, frustration, fear, sorrow, anxiety, worry or panic. Even something as minor as a fender-bender or a slow-speed parking lot accident can be enough to create emotion. Try to remain calm.

 When you are in an accident, the first thing you need to realize is that insurance companies

are the ones who typically investigate the accident to determine fault—so don't assume or admit that you are the guilty party. Being in an emotional state, or in a state of shock, can skew your perception of the accident. Let them do their job.

Next, call the police. Once they are on their way, exchange insurance information with the other driver. You should have your insurance information in the glove compartment to give the other party. Make sure to get proof of insurance from the other driver. If they have the necessary information available at the scene, call immediately to verify that they do have coverage. Just because the paper says they are covered doesn't mean their insurance is current.

For most states, unless there's bodily injury, you should remove the vehicle from the road. You can get a ticket for obstruction of traffic if you keep your car on the road when there's no personal injury. Remove your car to a safe place and proceed to work out the details with the other party as you await the arrival of the police.

Tow trucks dispatched by the police are under contract with the police. They will tow your vehicle to their impound lot and charge you a considerable amount to keep it there. (In fact, that's how most tow companies make their money—through storage from accidents. They make more money from storing your vehicle than from towing it.)

Instead, have a company tow the vehicle to your repair facility. Most repair facilities allow cars to remain there, free of charge, while the insurance company details are resolved. This will save you hundreds of dollars in storage fees.

If the police dispatch a towing company to the scene, you have the right to ask them to tow it to your home or to your repair shop. Do *not* allow them to tow it to their impound lot. If they do, you'll pay exorbitantly for it.

How to Manage Being Stuck in Traffic

The one thing you want to avoid is becoming trapped behind the car in front of you. The way I avoid that is to stop far enough behind that I can still see their rear tires touching the pavement. That way, I can maneuver around it if I need to.

You've heard of, or perhaps have been a part of, a pile up where one car rams into the car in front of them and it causes a domino effect. If you leave enough space between you and the car in front of you, you're not trapped; you can swing your car to either side and avoid being rammed from behind.

Sometimes traffic jams simply cannot be avoided. That's another reason to keep more than a quarter tank of gas in your car. You don't want to run out at a time like that.

Always watch your temperature gauge when you're stopped in traffic. Most cars are designed to be able to idle indefinitely—even with the air conditioning on. Still, you need to watch that gauge. If you notice your engine heating up, roll your windows down and turn off the air conditioning.

Traffic jams happen in the winter, as well. Some states require you to have a safety kit in your vehicle. The kit usually contains items like bottled water, a blanket, and a flashlight. It's not a bad idea. You never know when you'll be caught in traffic, or how long it will take to clear the roads.

How to Drive on Snow and Ice

Snow and ice certainly provide challenges to drivers. When driving on snow you need increased traction. That's why four-wheel-drive vehicles (or front-wheel-drive vehicles) get around better—simply because of their superior traction.

In deep snow, one tip that might come in handy is to lower the air pressure in your tires to about 25 pounds of pressure. You still won't be able to drive fast, but since there's more rubber on the road, you'll notice an improvement in your ability to negotiate snowy road conditions. However, only do this as a temporary emergency option. You may have to get your tire pressure monitors reset at your local shop after this procedure.

We learned years ago to gently pump the brakes in the snow, but the best advice I can offer is to drive as though you had an egg under the gas and brake pedals. Accelerate slowly and brake gently. Don't push on the pedals too strongly. You'll break the eggs!

Buying a used car can be risky business. Let me offer some strategies that might prove helpful in that situation.

First, do your homework. Look online, read consumer magazines, peruse some used car lots, investigate the For Sale ads in your newspaper and check out Kelly Blue Book for reasonable pricing. Take all the time you need to figure out exactly what you're interested in—make, model and even options.

Once you've narrowed your search, it's time to find that perfect vehicle—whether you intend to buy from an individual or a car dealership. Study the car, walk around it, and look at it from different angles. When you finish assessing the cosmetic aspects, then sit behind that steering wheel. Touch everything you can touch. Check out the wipers, the radio, the heat and air, the glove box and the lights. Make sure everything works, including turn signals, power windows, power locks, power seats, rear wipers, and so on.

If everything checks out, let the seller know you'd like to take about 45 minutes to an hour to road test this car. If they want to ride with you, that's fine, but make sure they're willing for you to spend the time you need.

Most people drive the car around the block or spend ten minutes driving up the road and back and say, "I'll take it"—but not you. You're too savvy for that. During your test drive, listen to the vehicle. Notice the way it feels, handles and steers. You don't have to be an automotive mechanic to know if something is not quite right.

If you hear a noise that concerns you, or there's a shake or shimmy in the steering, or anything else that doesn't quite seem right, make note of it. Spend time driving both on the freeway at highway speeds and in town at normal speeds. See how the vehicle take corners, slows, stops, accelerates—just as you would drive the vehicle on any given day.

Use your senses. Don't play the radio. Make sure the radio plays, then turn it off and listen. Use your five senses to note if anything seems abnormal.

If everything checks out, move to the next step—take it to an ASE-certified technician for a used-car inspection. This will include having a trained technician inspect the exterior and interior of the car, take it for a drive, bring it back into the bay and raise it up to do a more thorough inspection. The technician will know exactly the kinds of things to look for, the kinds of things that could signal a future problem. And when you get an "all clear" from someone who truly knows what they're doing, it will give you great confidence.

Through this process, the ASE-certified technician can help you make a decision about repairs that may need to be done now or in the near future and can tell you the costs of those repairs.

That will give you greater wisdom and leverage in making an offer to the seller. Once you decide to buy this particular car, you're ready for the final step—making the deal.

You should not talk about price, or make any offer until you have taken all these steps. Then you'll be able to approach the seller and tell them, "I'd like to buy this car. I've had it inspected and here is the estimate of the items that need attention in order to get it to a condition I'd be satisfied with. With that in mind, I'm willing to pay this amount for it—and if that's agreeable with you, I'm ready to buy it today."

THAT is the right way to buy a vehicle. Constrain your emotions, have a certified technician inspect it and know what you are getting into before you make an offer. By following this process, you will save yourself from some unpleasant surprises that could cost you a lot of money.

How to Find a Good Repair Shop

If you're moving out of your current area, one of the best actions you could take in finding a reliable new repair shop is to ask your current one. Most shops are in some kind of network or association and may know a good shop in the area where you're relocating.

If you're looking to find a reliable repair shop in your current locale, here are some tips about finding one you'll be happy with. Do some investigation. Ask others if they're satisfied with their shops. Check with your local Better Business Bureau.

When you've narrowed down your choices, move to the next step. Make an appointment for something relatively simple and easy—a tire rotation, or an oil change. When you take your car in, tell them you'll wait for it.

While you're waiting, look and listen. You can learn an awful lot when you do that.

While that service is being performed, pay attention to how employees interact with each other and with the other customers. Notice how they answer the phone. If possible, watch the way they handle your car. It won't take long before you arrive at an opinion about how professionally they run their shop. That can go a long way in helping you make a decision.

Find out if their technicians are certified and if they are required to participate in continuing education/training. Ascertain to what extent they service your particular make and model. Do they have the software to communicate with the computer systems on your vehicle? Do they have the specialized tools your car may require?

Ask them if they utilize any system of reminders to let you know when it's time for service. Do they have a schedule in place to keep your car well maintained?

Compare the shops you visit. Make an informed decision and choose the one that best meets your needs.

Five Questions to Ask a Shop

If you are not able to visit the repair shop, a phone call may need to suffice. If so, here are five simple questions you can ask any shop. As a word of caution, let me say that it's extremely dangerous to choose a shop based on their pricing. There's too much room for misunderstanding and manipulation if price is your only criteria. That's why I advise you to ask these questions and compare the answers you receive:

1. What is your warranty?
2. Do you offer a money-back guarantee?
3. Are your technicians ASE-Certified and do you have any ASE Master Technicians?
4. Do you provide a free round-trip shuttle or loaner vehicle?

5. What happens if I have trouble when you're
   closed?

These five simple questions will successfully point

you to the best shop in your area.

Concluding Comments

These instructions were designed as a guide for laypeople who may not have automotive experience. I trust they have been helpful and beneficial.

However, we do have additional resources available. Visit our website at www.AAtheShop.com. We have a national audience and try to provide ongoing instruction and insights people can apply to their own automotive issues. We have a number of blogs and videos on our site that deal with a variety of issues from head gaskets to heating systems and almost everything in between!

We are currently updating our blogs with video and pictures. We're going to provide video links and adding information on an ongoing basis. There will be guidelines and checklists for what to look for and what to avoid in purchasing a used vehicle, how to tell if it's a lemon or a gem.

Plus, we would like to get this book into the hands of as many as we can as a helpful guide to keep in your glove box for instant access—especially the troubleshooting sections.

We've designed this book to serve as a great gift for anyone who needs to understand more about their cars—for instance, a son or daughter getting their first car, or people who have never had to care for a vehicle before. We believe this is a great guide to understanding your Subaru, or other vehicle, and how to make it last longer with quality service.

Before closing, since we are so customer-oriented, I'd like to invite readers to make comments and suggestions by contacting us by phone, e-mail, or on our website so we can consider and incorporate any consumer interests we've overlooked. We're here for you.

Kurt Adler

A&A The Shop

www.AAtheShop.com

(907) 562-3919

4617 Old Seward Hwy,

Anchorage, AK 99503

www.AAtheShop.com

APPENDIX I: Head Gasket Solutions

From mid-1999 to 2004, we started seeing head gasket issues on some of the engines. We noted frequent problems with oil and/or coolant leaking from these head gaskets. Since many of these cars were still under factory warranty, we sent them to the Subaru dealer, who took care of the issues. Subaru's head gasket drive train warranty is five years, or 60,000 miles.

After the cars were out of warranty, we began working on these head gasket issues, but were having difficulty keeping our original 24-month, 24,000 mile warranty when we used factory Subaru head gaskets. It became obvious that we could no longer use those parts if we wanted to continue to honor our warranty.

I decided to take this issue to my good friend, John Hogan, from Northeast Imported Parts and Accessories, and we started brainstorming.

John, an awesome communicator and negotiator, is a great asset and representative for his company. He said, "You spec out that engine and let us know exactly where it's leaking, how it's leaking, compression, temperatures and based on your specifications, we'll see what we can do to get a head gasket built for you."

That's what we did. We painstakingly took the engines apart to investigate and determine the cause of the problem with the factory head gaskets.

At that time, Subaru utilized a single-layer head gasket. Previously, they used a multi-layered stainless steel head gasket, which was quite good. Knowing that Subaru had manufactured a really good head gasket, and discovering that the design seemed to be one of the major issues, Northeast went to one of their vendors and had a head gasket designed and built for us. This new product was based on the tri-metal stainless steel head gasket on the previous phase-one engines. We were ecstatic at how well the new head gasket performed.

But we didn't just leave it there. After about three or four years of testing, we took it a step further. They beefed up that head gasket to make it even better. We've been operating for two years on the second generation of that head gasket, and have had no problems whatsoever. Now these gaskets are being used nationally—even by some Subaru dealers. Northeast did a great job. Together, we saw something that wasn't working and we found a unique way to solve the issue.

This has helped other independents businesses, as well. Communication between this network of automotive repair establishments helps all of us. And when we have access to a great company like Northeast, we all benefit.

We're all working together towards a better industry.

APPENDIX II: BG Products

We use BG products and incorporate them into every factory maintenance service we do. It's an additive we put in the oil each time.

Basic oil has an API rating. API stands for American Petroleum Institute. Certain car manufacturers have to meet a minimum API rating for the oil in their vehicles. When you add a BG product to those oils—whether it's crankcase oil, engine oil, transmission or brake fluid, gear lube, or differential—it beefs up the API rating. By adding these products, we increase the oil quality, whether it's conventional or synthetic, and BG products raise it to higher standards.

What that means for the consumer is that it minimizes wear on the engine and other components. It does this by reducing friction, so your engine doesn't have to work as hard.

Using BG products is a factor in our ability to offer such a great, better than 24-carat gold warranty. Using these additives with every service adds years to the life of your vehicle. Plus, since BG stands behind its products, they will provide money toward repairs or replacement, when appropriate. They will help make it right! That gives our customers added confidence.

But that's not all. They also offer a roadside assistance package, which covers towing, flat tire repair, and lockout, as well—and at no added cost to the customer. These are some of the reasons we became a BG shop. We like the no-nonsense way they do business. It's just another benefit we add for our customers.

APPENDIX III: KYB Struts

Let's talk about everybody's favorite subject—struts. Seriously, though struts are important, few people realize *how* important they are for their vehicles. The ones I want to introduce you to are KYB struts. KYB stands for Kayaba, a manufacturer of struts used by Subaru. KYB struts are amazing—especially for Alaska. Kayaba carefully researches the equipment they manufacture and have come up with an exceptional product.

What are struts? A strut is a modified shock with hydraulics. Shocks that use an over-spring hydraulic valve assembly are called struts. These springs differentiate it from a shock absorber, which has no over-spring. Therefore, struts provide that comfortable driving experience you enjoy. When functioning properly, they also positively affect the wear and tear on the car and its braking system.

KYB struts are rated for five years or 50,000 miles. In extreme driving conditions, the primary valve actuates between 1,500 and 1,900 times every mile. That can add up to 95 million valve actuations. It is recommended that they get replaced. This valve is responsible for keeping the tire on the road, which contributes to handling and control. It prevents excessive tire and brake wear, as well as ball joint and suspension wear. It also decreases the stopping distance, which could be instrumental in preventing an accident. What used to take six feet to stop now takes thirty! Therefore, it becomes a safety issue as well.

This is just one more reason to get regular maintenance for your car. Unless you have a technician carefully checking your braking system and struts, you may not realize they're wearing until it's too late. Struts can be expensive, but driving without proper struts can cost you more in the long run.

APPENDIX IV: Extended Warranties

First, extended warranties are all over the board. A dealership typically offers two types. One is the type the manufacturer offers, so if I bought a Subaru, it would be a Subaru extended warranty. If I bought a GM, it would be a GM extended warranty. The dealership also offers an "after-market extended warranty." That is usually serviced by a company whose sole product is extended warranties.

For whatever reason, most after-market extended warranty companies are located or originated in the St. Louis area. The St. Louis Better Business Bureau and the St. Louis Attorney General spend significant time dealing with these companies because of consumer complaints.

ConsumerAffairs.com says, "From what we've heard, we suspect that most extended warranties are a waste of money that could be better spent on performing exquisite maintenance, still the best insurance of trouble-free motoring." They also said, "Sixty-five percent (or more than 8,000) *Consumer Reports* readers surveyed by the Consumer Reports National Research Center in the winter of 2011 said they spent significantly more for a new car warranty than they got back in repair cost savings." That is very common.

(*http://www.consumeraffairs.com/news04/2005/extended_w arranty.html*)

There are even conventions for these companies that teach how to sell an extended warranty. The following information is from the website, *WarrantyInnovations.com*. The whole purpose of the convention, throughout all their breakout sessions and their main course, was this—and this is in the notes of the meeting!

"The discussion will also include ways to leverage systems and data to drive extended warranty sales, how to build a recurring revenue stream with extended warranties in maintenance, lower costs, and claims against your program and how to better work with your insurance and our administrator."

That information clearly states that their intent is to sell more warranties and reduce the number of claims. Extended warranties are a contract, and I learned a long time ago that contracts are usually written in favor of those who write them.

Without question, extended warranty contracts are not good for the consumer. Can you find people who have been able to save money in buying an extended warranty? Yes, you can. The response rate, according to *Consumer Reports,* is about one in five—so about 20% said they had a net savings.

The *Consumer Reports* study basically says that when you're buying a car, it is better *not* to buy an extended warranty, but instead use those dollars to maintain your vehicle. In the survey, respondents cited warranty costs of $1,000 on average that provided benefits of $700—a $300 loss. Forty-two percent of extended warranties were never used, and only about a third of all respondents used their plan to cover a serious problem.

There are also exclusions from coverage by an extended warranty. So, even though you purchased the warranty, you're still going to have to pay for repairs that are not covered. Beware, because there is a lot of fine print in those contracts. Read it carefully, if you're considering purchasing a warranty.

Most extended warranties give the warranty company the option of putting used parts on your car. So if your transmission goes out, instead of getting a new transmission, you could get a used one—one out of a salvage yard or from a recycler. It's their choice, not yours. That's scary, but it saves them money.

About The Author

Kurt Adler and his wife, Joan, live with their children in Anchorage, Alaska where they own and operate A&A The Shop. Kurt is a graduate of the University of Alaska Anchorage where he learned automotive, diesel and welding skills. He was active in school government and was a member of Phi Theta Kappa.

Kurt's interests include fabrication of automotive parts, fishing, boating, prospecting, shrimping, as well as traveling around Alaska and other states.

He has been in the automotive repair business since 1996, working exclusively on Subaru. He is a member of the Anchorage Chamber of Commerce, the Better Business Bureau (BBB), Automotive Service Association (ASA), Automotive Service Excellence (ASE) and the National Federation of Independent Business (NFIB). Check him out at www.AAtheShop.com, or call him at (907) 562-3919 for your automotive questions.

Alaska's Independent Subaru Service

4617 Old Seward Hwy
Anchorage, AK 99503
(907) 562-3919

11135 Ashley Park Ln
Eagle River, AK 99577
(907) 696-2096

Store Hours: Mon-Sat 7am-5:30pm
Shuttle Service: Mon-Sat 7:30am - 3:00pm

Made in the USA
San Bernardino, CA
03 March 2015